MW01632141

ANYONE CAN WRITE PICTURE BOOKS

HERE'S HOW TO WRITE ONES KIDS LOVE

ADAM WALLACE

KRUEGER WALLACE PRESS

ANYONE CAN WRITE PICTURE BOOKS ... Here's how to write ones kids LOVE!

First published in the Year of the Teeny Tiny Ant Baby, 2024
by
Krueger Wallace Press

Email: wally@adam-wallace-books.com or visit
www.adam-wallace-books.com or visit
the dentist. They'll make your teeth SHINE!

ABN: 31 260 817 318

ISBN: 978-1-7637453-0-8

Printed by Amazon KDP.

Do not use this book as a blender or a microwave oven.

This book is not a UFO or an OJ.

OPEN WIDE, WHAT'S INSIDE?

WARNING

Before we begin, there's something you should know about me. I write books **FOR CHILDREN!**

Not for booksellers, although it's great if they like them too.

Not for parents, although it's great if they like them too.

Not even for teachers or librarians, although it's especially great if they like them too.

Here's the thing. If kids ***LOVE*** a book, adults will find a way to like it too. They will take everything they say they do or don't like about books for children, and they will twist it so it fits these books.

Or, which is even better, they'll buy it just because their child is or students are so excited!

Because children are the key! Won't somebody think of the children!

As adults we're mostly set in our ways, our likes and dislikes, our pretty much everythings. But kid's books open that up, open ***us*** up. If our child is over the top excited to read a book, we are going to find a way to enjoy that book ... unless you're a heartless monster, in which case you would say, "This book is rubbish, choose something else."

All of this is to say, you're a heartless monster ... wait. No. That's not it ... I hope! It's to say that if you say you want to write books for children, actually write books for children!

THEY are your audience. No one else. The others will all come along for the ride.

This was driven home to me after a launch I did, for Jamie Brown is NOT Rich (*named after a real Jamie Brown, RIP*).

We were at dinner after, celebrating, and my step-mother Bronwen said, "Adam. Your speech."

"Yes?" I replied, leaning forward, eager to receive the praise that was surely coming my way.

"It was ***TERRIBLE***," Bronwen said (*and that is censored ...*). I was slightly distraught, but then she explained why. The thing is, I aimed some bits at the kids, some at the adults, some somewhere in-between, so it became a mish-mash of a speech.

"Speak to the kids," Bronwen advised. "The adults will come along, and if they don't, who cares? The book is for the kids! If they want it, the parents will buy it to keep them quiet!"

In her brutal but honest way, Bronwen changed how I thought about writing. Kids are now first, second, and third through tenth in the top ten most important people I think about when writing a kid's book.

I hope, by the end of this book, you feel the same. I am going to fill Bronwen's shoes here. I will be brutally honest, because if we're writing for children, we must take an example from them ... and zombies.

Be honest. Be authentic. Be real.

We always get told to think about our audience, and yet we write a mish-mash of stories aimed at parents, teachers, publishers, booksellers and sometimes even children.

Flip it. You write for children, so write for children. Market to adults, they have money, but write for children.

To help with this, I will give you all I have learned from 25 years of being a writer ***for*** children, from hundreds of rejections to New York Times Bestseller, from self-publishing and struggling to sell one book to having sold over 10 million picture books and counting.

But these are merely my experiences. As Bruce Lee says, "Absorb the information. Discard what's useless. Take what's useful. Make it your own."

So here we go. Get ready to discard and absorb.

Come on. Let's create magic!

One final thing. All the pictures in here are in Black and White. This isn't very bright and colourful, but lets me get this book to you for $10 cheaper. The end.

INTRODUCTION

I was having breakfast with a few people at a mastermind event. They were an incredible group, and the chats were so inspiring.

At one point, it was suggested one of the people there should write a picture book. "Go on," someone said. "It's only 400 words."

I said to myself (*or so I thought*), "Yeah. 400 ***GOOD*** words."

Mike, sitting next to me, overheard and laughed. This is such a common misconception though.

Someone else once said to me, "I wrote a story, and because I can't write, it became a children's book."

And he worked for a charity and was asking me for money! (**Side note: I gave him money ...*)

I wrote my first picture book because someone dared me to, saying, "Anyone can write a picture book!"

The thing is, anyone ***CAN*** write a picture book. Absolutely. But can they write a picture book that lasts years, decades, more? Can they write a picture book kids want to hear again and again and again? A picture book that entertains and inspires?

That part's not so easy.

So what's the magic? And how can you capture it and put it in a bottle ... or a book, at least!

Creating picture books is an amazing experience, from thinking up and writing the story to seeing it come to life in the expert hands of an illustrator, to seeing it in the world, to seeing the joy it brings children.

Is it easy to write a picture book? Absolutely! Is it easy to write a good, let alone AMAZING, picture book? ***NOT AT ALL!!!*** Or at least, it wasn't until now! Because you are about to get the inside scoop from a **New York Times, Amazon and USA Today bestselling author** who has sold over **10 MILLION** picture books and **11 MILLION** books in total!

SO WHAT IS IN THIS BOOK?
IS THERE A KITTEN? IS THERE A HOOK?

No. There isn't. I wish there was a kitten. But there is a ***HEAP*** of info, tips and tricks! By the end of this book you will:

1. Know everything you need to know about word counts, page lengths, age groups and more.

2. Understand why character is so important in picture books.

3. Be inspired to use movie structures to help you write picture books!

4. Write with the illustrations in mind!

5. Be able to weigh up the pros and cons of writing in rhyme and write ***AMAZING*** rhyme!

6. Have the secret sauce! The structure that super successful picture books use!

7. Learn layout tricks that bring amazing energy and anticipation to your picture book!

8. Have discovered new ideas on how to ***GET*** new ideas for picture books!

9. Get heeeeeaps of ***FREE*** bonus picture book ideas you can use right away!

10. Know the answers to many questions people ask about editing and submitting picture books.

And that's not all! Actually, it kind of is, but that's a lot right? And, as they say, always leave 'em wanting more! But this won't just be reading for you, you'll need to get writing as well.

Yep, homework will be assigned. This means you will leave this course with, at the very least, new ideas and templates and thoughts on picture books. At best, you will have taken those ideas and written an awesome picture book ... or books!

First up, to kick things off, it is really important for ***YOU*** to think about what ***YOU*** want to get out of this book. Why do ***YOU*** want to read it? And, more to the point, why do ***YOU*** want to write picture books?

Having a strong why is really important in completing anything. It helps you find the time. It helps you push through parts that are hard. Certainly, in writing and getting picture books published, you have to push through so many things - getting the words right, the rhythm, the story, there will be rejections, bad reviews, children walking away as you read to them ... sigh.

Having a strong ***WHY*** will really help you move past all of that and get to the exhilarating moment of having ***YOUR*** picture book in ***YOUR*** hands.

Or, even better, seeing a kid you don't know getting delight out of your book.

There will be some technical things in this book, but a lot of it will be aiming to bring stories out of you, to help you find the picture book you've been aching to write.

So grab your notebook (*paper or computer*), look inside (*the notebook* ***AND*** *yourself*) and do some writing. This is your time, for you, so write what comes out, no edits. Trust your soul. Here's your question.

WHAT DO YOU WANT TO GET OUT OF THIS BOOK?

Yep, write down what you would like to learn from this book. And check back once you're finished. If there's anything that wasn't covered, email me at **wally@adam-wallace-books.com** and I will do my best to fill in the gaps!

Next, write down reasons why ***you*** want to write ***picture books!***

Is it to bring joy to kids?

To tell a story that's been burning inside of you?

To have a story for ***your*** kids or grandkids?

Whatever it is, write it down! Let it out! There is no wrong here, only what you think and feel. And again, this is for you. You can show other people, but you don't have to.

It can just be for you. So go for it. I'll see you on the other side.

A LITTLE BIT ABOUT ME

Okay, I'm going to keep this as brief as possible. Which isn't always easy for me ... which is why picture books are not always easy for me!

Which is why I had to work out the formula, and once I did, it changed everything. But that's for later. I want to give a little intro to me and why I am the person to guide you through this process of creating a magical picture book.

It all started, really, back when I was a kid, and my step-dad was a teacher-librarian. Our house was filled with books, and we were always read to.

My favorites were Roald Dahl, Dr Seuss, and Bill Peet. You may not know Bill Peet, but he was a genius. I will be referring to his books as we go through the course, and they are definitely worth checking out.

My grandmother also wrote picture books, some of which were even illustrated by Mirka Moira (*If you don't know Mirka Moira, look her up as well, she's very cool!*)

So I've always had a massive fondness for picture books, and certainly when I started writing, like a lot of people, that was what I wrote first. There really is a magical feeling around creating an entire story in a limited number of words.

And for those who think picture books are easy because they're short, the hardest book I ever wrote was **TEN** pages, with **FIVE** words on each page.

Almost killed me! Literally! But when I got it done, it was ***SUCH*** a thrill!

Anyway, as I mentioned earlier, I was eventually dared as an adult to write a picture book. As soon as I did, a world opened up before me. A world that has changed everything. A world of writing every day.

So that's me. Everyone will have a different story as to how they got into picture books, or why they want to write them. Mine was drilled into me from early childhood and I still love reading them now.

In the end, how we got here matters but doesn't matter. We're here. We're writing them. And at some stage, years from now, there will be kids who remember our books from when they were little.

And to have that impact, to have that influence? Wow, just wow.

We'll get to dissecting picture books and making the whole process, from idea to publication, simpler in a moment! First, aside from my story of why I like picture books, I better show how I've gone writing them, because just liking them isn't enough.

We don't want financial advice from someone who's broke, or relationship advice from someone in a terrible relationship, so we don't want writing advice from someone without a good track record either.

So here's mine, right now, in September, 2024.

ADAM WALLACE - THE EVIDENCE

I've done picture books with companies in Australia, America, South Korea and Slovenia.

I have had picture books on the **New York Times Bestseller List** for a combined 212 weeks and five books that made it to **Number One.**

How to Catch a Leprechaun has twice been **Number 1** on the Amazon Bestseller List (out of **33,000,000** or so books) and ***How to Catch the Easter Bunny*** got to Top 3 as well.

My picture books have been on the **USA Today Bestseller List.**

How to Catch the Easter Bunny was read on the White House Lawn.

How to Catch a Leprechaun was a question on Jeopardy USA. Twice.

Over 170 books published.

Over 11 million books sold.

My picture books made it to the DJ Khaled, Rihanna, and Kim, Kourtney and Khloe Kardashian households - none of these were delivered personally, unfortunately, but the posts online thrilled me!

Okay, so that's me, but this is about you. Oh yes, it's ***ALL*** about you now, which some people will love, and some people will cringe away from!

But, as Mum always says, "You get out of it what you put into it."

So here are my two asks of you:

1. Read this book with good energy, looking for ways to make your books the best they can be. Not everything I say will strike a chord, but there might be some gold. Be alert and you will discover it!

2. PLAY! We're writing children's books! It's not digging ditches or cleaning toilets. Take your writing seriously, but don't take yourself seriously.

We don't work the piano. We don't work a game. **This is writing!** It's a privilege, a joy, a delight. Work hard, but have fun while you do it.

And whenever you hear someone saying, "Oh, writing is really hard. It's a slog," say to yourself, "You don't get it."

Because they don't.

PS I will show pictures from a number of my own picture books as we go along, mostly because I'm not 100% sure of the legalities of showing others ... if I do, you'll know I finally checked it out!

SECTION 1

SOME PICTURE BOOK NUMBERS

PAGES? WORDS? AGE GROUPS?

First up, let me say this ... I think rules are meant to be broken! But I ***also*** think you need to know the rules before you break them!

So let's break it down like a rap star! Let's break it down like a hammer on a window. Let's break it down like a good cop/bad cop. Let's break it down like ... ah, let's just get to it.

HOW MANY WORDS SHOULD YOUR PICTURE BOOK BE?

As I said, I have written a picture book that was around 50 words long. I have also written picture books that were near on 900 words, some 400, and the most recent one I did was 275 words!

The Lorax, by Dr Seuss, one of the greatest picture books of all time, is around 1800 words long.

The Arrival, by Shaun Tan, has ***NO*** words!

In most submission guidelines, publishers say picture books should be under 500 words long.

So what can ***you*** do? One thing, and one thing alone, especially in your first draft.

Write the story your instinct wants to write. See what comes out and how many words it is. That first draft can be any length you like. As you write more and more picture books (*and using some techniques we will go through in this book*), your instinct will start to find the length you want anyway.

Then look at who you would like the book to be for, what age group.

Then look at other books for that age group and how many words they are (*on average*).

Then look at Publisher submission guidelines.

Until you are Shaun Tan or Dr Seuss, if your book doesn't fit submission guidelines for word count for that age group, it won't be picked up unless it is the most amazing book ever.

Like, ***EVER!***

In the meantime, until you reach that level, or if you want to self-publish, write whatever you want to write. But, if you're submitting it, work to the Publisher Guidelines. Does it mean the publisher is right that a book has to be a certain length?

Nope, not at all.

But it does mean it's right for them, and if you want them to take your book, that's the right you have to fit into ... for now!

One interesting thing parents have said to me is that when a book is too long, they will skip bits when reading to their kids at bedtime. So that is something to consider as well.

My recommendation, when you're starting out especially, is **the shorter the better**. If you can keep it under 500 words and have a concise, full story, you are well on the way to picture book success.

HOMEWORK

Look at some of your favorite picture books (*and some of your **non**-favorite picture books*), and count the words (*or Google them, for famous books!*).

Do they fit with what publishers are asking for? Are they mostly under 500 words? Do the ones that seem to be aimed at very young children have lower word counts?

Take a sample and you may start to notice trends.

HOW MANY PAGES ARE PICTURE BOOKS?

Again, similar to word count, this is going to change depending on the age group. Books for very young children, say 0-2 years old, will be much shorter than books for 4-7 year olds.

Most picture books will be a multiple of four pages ... usually 24 or 32.

This is due to printing procedures and costs, although this is changing with the advent of digital printing, where books generally just have to be an even number of pages.

This number of pages in a book also includes all the imprint pages, half-title pages, dedication pages, blank pages and potentially more!

What this means is your actual story doesn't have to be a multiple of four pages. A 32 page book will often have a 26-28 page story.

Unless you are self-publishing, and unless you are laying it out for the publisher, don't worry about page count for now (*although it is a nice way to get your word count working well*). Aim for that 500 word mark, and you will generally be fine.

HOMEWORK

Check out some of the picture books you looked at in the last homework, and see how many pages the book is ... then see how many pages the actual story is!

For bonus points, look at how many words are on each page, and how they are laid out. Note the similarities and differences, both between books and even within books. See if it changes how you feel about the book, and how you read the book.

Do different numbers of words on a page make it feel different reading it to yourself and reading it out loud?

Play!!!!!!!

WHAT AGE GROUP DO PICTURE BOOKS TARGET?

It's a pretty small age group range ... you know, just 0-100!!! Yep, picture books are written for newborns, they're written for toddlers, kindergarten kids, primary school kids, high school kids, and even for adults!

Think I'm joking? I am ... ***NO I'M NOT!*** I bet there's at least one picture book for adults you can think of, and if not, look it up.

The most famous one I know sold hundreds of thousands of copies, if not more, and was even read online by Samuel L. Jackson and Noni Hazlehurst!

There was once a picture book that one a big award here in Australia, the picture book of the year, which at that stage was (*and may still be*) for ages 0-18. The author never planned for it to be for younger kids, but when it won, every primary school bought it, as they do each year.

They should have done some research.

Imagine the teachers' and librarians' surprise when they discovered swear words, death themes, graphic images, all ***AMAZING*** and worthy of its win, but shows that not all picture books are for young children.

Picture books come in all shapes and sizes and can be aimed at all different age groups. On the next page are some I've done, and their target age group.

Target age: 3-7
Word count: ~420

Target age: 2-6
Word count
varied, ten
personalized stories

Target age: 5-9
Word count: ~900

Target age: 0-3
Word count: 50

So as you can see, the age range can vary, though mine are sort of similar, and the top right one, personalized stories done through the incredible Hooray Heroes, is quite different. In fact, that was a different job altogether, and quite the story! Let me tangent ...

So one day, I got an email from Mic, who said he had a children's book publishing company in Slovenia, and did I want to do some work with them!

Yep, I totally thought it was a scam. A) I have had scam emails before, and B) I had never heard of Slovenia, so assumed this was a Nigerian Prince type of thing!

But they gave a link to their website, which looked ***SO GOOD***, and wanted to have a meeting.

So I Googled Slovenia, was entranced, and agreed to the meeting.

The people at Hooray Heroes (**www.hoorayheroes.com**) were like the nicest ever, and I was in, agreeing to work with them.

As I said, they do personalized books, and the first one I worked on was a Christmas one. I wrote thirty poems, of varying but similar length, and people would go in, choose the ten poems they wanted, and that would be what they got.

But the magic didn't stop there! Each spread had one poem and an out of this world picture, done by the awesome Marko Renko (*@markorenko on Instagram*), and the buyer would personalize the main character, choosing hair color, hair style, eye color, gender, freckles, glasses and more!

And the results are insanely good (*even in black and white!*)

This is actually my all-time favorite pic in any of my books.

Anyway, I digress, as I am apt to do, but I wanted to show how wide-spread our opportunities are. I ended up visiting Slovenia, thanks to Hooray Heroes, and it is now my second favorite place in the world.

The other thing is that Hooray Heroes now do these picture books ***FOR ADULTS!!!***

So, getting back on track, what influences the age group a picture book is aimed at? Well, some things are:

Language - simpler language for younger age groups. Don't shy away from putting in one or two hard words though! This is how vocabulary is built! But too many hard words is frustrating ... it's a fine balance.

Length - This can totally vary, but as a rule books for younger kids are shorter. Less words. Less pages. Less easily destroyed. Apparently young kids have a short attention span! Who knew???

Humor - Books aimed at younger kids generally have physical humor. As kids get older, they still love the physical stuff, but wordplay can be built in as well.

Themes - Books for younger kids have very simple themes. As they mature, the themes can become more complex, and involve things like losing a pet, getting a younger sibling, etc.

Lessons - This is a really interesting one! Kids in Grade 6 would be very unlikely to choose a picture book from a shop, but they can still be used in classrooms to pass on lessons!

And, in the end, after all that, it is still a generalization! You may have an older kid who loves the feel and humor of picture books, or an advanced younger kid who is able to get different types of humor!

But these generalizations really help tighten your story. Having an idea of who the book is for will guide you in other areas, such as those mentioned above.

The easiest way to get an idea is to read, read, read, to see what sort of books kids of all ages are loving. And ask kids ***why*** they like them, don't just assume!

HOMEWORK

Find out what books kids of different age groups are loving, and why! See if you can notice any trends.

Is it the humor? Are they often a specific length? Ask friends, teachers, parents, librarians, bookstore worker people, do online searches, and most importantly, as I said above, **ask children!**

Search for patterns. See what's working, then you have the choice to follow that path, or create a new path, but start from a base of knowledge.

Also look for books that cross age groups. Maybe 5 year olds ***AND*** 9 year olds love it. Maybe kids ***AND*** adults love it (*this is a **HUGE** sweet spot to aim for*).

SECTION 2

WHERE DID I COME FROM?

GETTING IDEAS FOR PICTURE BOOKS

HOW DO YOU COME UP WITH YOUR IDEAS?

This is the question I get asked the most by kids ... ***AND ADULTS!!!*** It's a really tricky one to answer, too, because ideas literally come from everywhere and anywhere, and picture books can be about anything!

Google a topic and picture book, and see what comes up!

Oranges picture book? Yep.

Car crash picture book? Yep!

Dogs? Cats? Sea cucumbers? Yep yep yep!

This is ***AMAZING!*** Because it means you can literally write about whatever pops into your creative brain!

The thing is, and it's kind of a little miracle, the more writing you do, the more ideas you will get. It's like they start appearing for you. This is because, as we write more, we get in the mode of exploring ideas, even if it is just stream of consciousness writing - in fact, this is the best type!

When you write in a stream of consciousness manner, whether that's morning pages (*See The Artist's Way, by Julia Cameron*), or warming up, or writing for fun, or how you actually write, doing this helps remove the blockages and barriers we put up.

When you remove those blockages and barriers, well, we're more open to seeing new ideas.

MAGIC!

But in saying that, there are techniques we can use as well, and again, the more we use these techniques, the more ideas will seem to appear for us.

In the next section, we will burrow into the importance of character in creating a picture book.

But for now, let's get random!

First, my top ways to get ideas for picture books, then some homework for you!

1. **Observe!** Watch people and animals and couples and groups and trees and everything! Observe different levels of status, how interactions play out, and then **imagine what might happen next**, or **what happened in the lead-up**, or imagine whatever pops into your head!

2. **Read!** The more picture books you read, the more you start to see the range of ideas and possibilities. Also, just because a theme has been done doesn't mean it's locked up. There are millions of books on bullying, and loss, and friendship. Read a book, then find a way to do that theme in your own unique way!

3. **Read!** Read other genres of books! Novels, non-fiction, philosophy, biographies, everything. From these, you not only see what ideas have been done, it can spark new ideas in you as well!

4. **Listen to songs!** Songs are an ***INCREDIBLE*** resource for ideas! They have torment and longing and inspiration and joy and sadness and everything in between. I listen to songs as though they could be in the soundtrack to the movie of my book, and work scenes or stories around that!

Not only this, songs often have a lovely structure of ups and downs, love and loss and more. Try applying a song structure to a story idea and see what happens.

5. **Listen to people who won't do it themselves!** You are a book creator. Seriously, ***SOOOOOOO*** many people will say to you one of three things ... over and over and over and over and over again!

"I have an idea for a book."

"You know what you should write about?"

"Oooooh, now that's a great idea for a story!"

A lot of times, these ideas or situations won't spark anything ... but sometimes they will! A recent book I wrote that got picked up by Scholastic started with this exact thing! And you might not write the exact idea someone had, but it might spark something else for you.

6. **Write Titles!** Just think of titles and write them down. Be as crazy as you like. You probably won't use most of them, but you only need one or two to spark some writing and it's a win!

7. There are NO bad ideas! Honestly, and especially when it comes to writing, there are no bad ideas. The thing is, we want every idea we have to be perfect and lead to the perfect story. ***It ain't that easy!*** You may come up with 50 ideas and write 30 stories before you hit on one that is ***THE*** one!

Stand-up comedians do hours of material for a ten minute set. **I have written over 4000 stories!** Be the same. Write down **waaaaay** more ideas and stories than you expect to publish. You're a writer. Write. And then, when you've written, write again! And ***AGAIN!***

Also, an idea you might think is rubbish or silly or crazy when you first get it may turn out to be the best story you have ever written, especially if you decide to just play with it and write it for fun, with no other expectations.

There are ***NO*** bad ideas. Give every idea a chance, and not only will you write some fun stories, it will make you more open to seeing ideas. If you refuse all but what you think are the best ideas, you are limiting yourself so much, and the ideas won't flow.

Again. You're a writer. Write.

HOMEWORK

So those are some ways I come up with ideas for picture books. Some may work for you, some may not. But the more things you try, the more books will fly! Now here are some other things you can try to get the imagination and inspiration flying!

1. Write down all the ways people annoy you. Go on. Have fun with it. Look for every little nit-picking way people tick you off. One word for each is enough, but you can write more. For me what came up was - Greedy. Negative. Indulgent. Complaining. Bullying. Needy.

People say children are little adults. I disagree. I think adults are big children. So all those themes are played out with kids as well as adults. I chose three of the above words, and I wrote The Share-a-not, Mac O'Beasty, and The Negatees. Three of my all-time favorites.

Give it a go. This is something comedians often do for their routines. In a picture book, you can write about a character with the negative trait that annoys you, then teach them the lesson and change them! Then give the book to that person without saying it's about them!

Okay, so write down **5 ways** (*more if you like*) that people get on your bad side.

What do they do?

How do they act?

Why does it annoy you?

Even if it's something like cutting you off in a car park, that can be used indirectly in a picture book - a bird who always gets the good spot in the nest by waiting to see where the other birds go, then jumping in!

Go! Have fun!

AWeSoMe!

Now write about a fictional character (*doesn't even have to be human, as with the bird example on the previous page*) who has that quality, but ***really exaggerate it!***

If they're mean, make them the meanest person ever! If they're selfish, take it to the extreme! See what comes out. It's easier to tone back than to go the other way!

This doesn't have to be a story. It can just be a character description! But if a story comes out, write that! Follow the energy!

(***NOTE: It is REALLY fun to totally exaggerate the negative quality***)

This is The Negatees, my excessively negative character!

2. Now flip it. What do you find funny or interesting? I find farts and gross humor funny, so wrote a story called ***Whoops***, with a kid who does a massive pop-off! I even did it as a uni assignment (*and got an A, thank you very much!*).

This then led to my first book, ***Better Out Than In,*** and with that reputation, a 9 book series (*with two spin-off series*) called ***Fartboy.***

So what do **YOU** find funny? It can just be a word (*slapstick, wordplay, farts, babies in tuxedos*) or it can be a sentence (*Seeing supermodels wobbling on high heels*). Write it all down!

Now, pick a couple of those things and write about them for 5 minutes. Play. Be silly. Be serious. Exaggerate.

See if a story starts to appear, or if it's just more thoughts. Whatever! Get that notebook or computer or notebook computer and get writing!

3. Check out the following storyboard! Draw it out in your notebook or do it up on your computer.

If you put 1 thing in each column, you get a story idea. If you put 5 things in each column like I have below ... that's over ***3,000 possible story ideas!*** More in each column, more ideas.

Then circle one thing in each column, from anywhere in the column, even if it doesn't match with the other things you select (*sometimes these are the most fun!*) and ... ***BANG!*** Story idea! Now write about it!

MAIN CHARACTER	SKILL/ POWER	NEMESIS	LOCATION	SITUATION/ PROBLEM

Now create your own storyboard.

This time enter any column headings you like.

Maybe the nemesis has a skill.

Maybe one column is Main Character's Best Friend.

Whatever you want that you think fills out a storyline!

You can even add extra columns if you want!

If you fill two boards, that's ***THOUSANDS OF IDEAS! MAYBE MILLIONS!***

SECTION 3

THE IMPORTANCE OF CHARACTER!

CHARACTER IS CRUCIAL!

A lot of people will tell you that story is the most important thing in a picture book, but I disagree. Story ***IS*** important, don't get me wrong, but ***I*** believe the most important thing in a picture book (*or any book, really*), depending on the style, of course, is character.

What do I mean by depending on the style? Well, for example, check out this one I did with James Hart ...

This was a series of fun pages with different animals popping off. So there was no central character. The character, in a way, was the events happening, the concept.

But if you're writing a **STORY** as opposed to a book, character is crucial. ***CRUCIAL, I SAY!*** Why? Well, let me elaborate!

CHARACTER DRIVES THE STORY/ PLOT!

You have a character, and that character wants something. They have an intention. Aaron Sorkin (*Who is a genius, by the way. His class on www. masterclass.com is a* ***must watch*** *for any writer*) talks about intention and obstacle being the key in TV shows. In picture books, it's the same.

Have a character that wants something, then don't let them have it ... or at least make it hard! A kid wants to go to the beach, parents won't let him. A dog wants a walk, but it's raining. A selfish kid has to share. A naughty kid gets in trouble for playing pranks, or doesn't get the response they are after.

CHARACTER PROVIDES CHANGE

When a character changes, or learns a lesson, or overcomes obstacles, that's a great start for a picture book. Kid can't do something at the start, keeps trying, does it at the end. ***BAM!*** Story arc!

CHARACTER PROVIDES OPTIONS

This is a fun one. See, most often a character will have an **external** goal, or intention ... they want to go to the beach; they want to play pranks; they want all the lollies; they want a puppy.

Often though, the **internal** goal is different ... and the character may not even realize this! They want to spend time with their parents, who are always busy. They want responses and attention on them. They can't eat lollies at home. They want a friend because the other kids tease them.

The great thing is, this means the end result isn't always what seemed necessary or what they wanted at the start, so you can do super cool twists, and the support players can change as well!

CHARACTER DRIVES A SERIES

Not always, but if you want to write a series, a ***HUUUUGE*** percentage of the time you need a great character.

Pig the Pug.
The Hippopotamus on the Roof.
The Pigeon on the Bus.
Charlie and Lola.
Winnie the Pooh.
Knuffle Bunny.
Pete the Cat, The Cat in the Hat, The Cat Wants Custard and many more cat and other books too.

Even something like Do NOT Open This Book, it's the character that drives the series (*and the great concept!*).

Having a great character people know and love means you can throw that character into any situation, and people know how they will respond ... which also means you can twist that around every now and then too!

CHARACTER PROVIDES SUPPORT CHARACTERS

This is one of the best bonuses of having a great character, because having a strong character allows you to create a great support cast. This is especially true once we start to think about what the support cast will bring out of the main character, and vice versa.

Perhaps the kid is brave and arrogant ... but scared of dogs. Right! Support cast. A dog, obviously. Or a kid who knows about the fear and uses it against them. The local dogcatcher who needs an apprentice. Already there are inklings of a storyline.

This also allows your character to overcome something. They're scared of dogs? Have them overcome that fear to protect their friend or save a dog. **BAM!**

It's nice to have support casts that bring out good and bad traits in your main character. One who is an obstacle to what they want, and one who is potentially the answer to their flaw. If the main character is selfish, have a generous character who subtly shows them the error of their ways.

And on that ...

CHARACTERS ARE FLAWED

In fact, they should be. In fact, they ***MUST*** be!!! Again, we want the character to change, and in the best stories, they change from a flawed character to someone who overcomes that flaw. This can often happen as they reach their internal goal.

Can you have a character who is perfect then gets a flaw and is awful at the end? Not an easy sell to a publisher ... but perhaps one who seems perfect, gains a flaw, then overcomes it could be a winner!

This also allows us to play with things, and have a character ***NOT*** overcome the flaw, and do it in a way that lets the reader see the way they could have done it, opening the book up for amazing discussions.

CHARACTER DRIVES LOCATIONS/ SITUATIONS

They sure do, and this is the fun one. Similar to what I talked about in the series bit, knowing your character allows you to throw them into many and varied locations and situations. It's also great to **use opposites** here because that introduces our obstacles!

Naughty character? Send them to a super strict school. Noisy character? Put them in a library or church or funeral! A kid who hates being the center of attention? Make it happen! Poor family? Get them among the snobby rich elite!

PUT YOUR CHARACTER WHERE THEY DON'T BELONG!

This allows them to either find something else in them, or charm their way out of a situation and win over their rival, Or they get in massive trouble and may not even learn the lesson, but we, the readers, do!

Using this technique is also amazing for creating support characters, where our main character brings things out of the support cast.

A loud character in a library? We have the librarian, other people in the library, the main character's family.

Naughty character at a strict school? Teachers, the principal, good students who are appalled, bad students who are inspired, the police, the kid's family, the dog that runs onto the school grounds, so many opportunities here!

HOMEWORK

Okay, get that notebook and that brain ready, it's time to create some characters! There are so many ways to do this, but we're going to do a couple of simple ones to start with.

Without really thinking about it, make up a character (*or more than one*) and 5 things about them. It can literally be anything, but it's great if at least one trait is a flaw. Here's a couple of examples:

1. **Boy. 6 years old. Hates cats. Scared of ants. Favorite food is bananas.**

2. **Monkey. Lives in a zoo. Hates bananas. Loves to read. Can't help stealing things.**

Okay! Your turn!

Great! Now think about two supporting characters you could throw in a story with your character. They can be surprising or super obvious. For mine:

1. **His mum, who's a crazy cat lady. His sister, who has an ant farm.**

2. **His best friend, the hippo next door. The zookeeper, who also loves to read and has lots of books.**

Awesome! And if you think of more than two, write them allllllll down! The more the better! You may end up even combining two of the characters into one.

Okay, so now, think up some simple scenarios. Again, using my examples:

1. His mum gets a new cat. He leaves out a honey sandwich in his bed. He brings a stray dog home.

2. The zookeeper gets a signed copy of War and Peace. Monkey escapes from the zoo and robs banks. Hippo drenches all the monkey's books.

Sooooooooo, what you have there are two very simple bases for not only a story, but potentially a series!

Each of those scenarios lends itself to a new book in the series!

And remember ... not every idea you brainstorm will come to fruition, but if you write fast and don't censor yourself, you never know what will come out. And the more you do, you get the opportunity to mix and match!

And don't stop at one and feel like your work is done. Do more, more I say!

NEVER WORK WITH CHILDREN AND ANIMALS

That's what they say, but animals are very popular in picture books. So for us, it's work ***WITH*** animals ... ***AND*** children!

WHAAAAAAAT???

I know. Crazy, right? But there are a few reasons animals are great characters (*and monsters too*).

1. Children feel more comfortable talking about an issue they're dealing with if it involves an animal (*or monster*) in a book. I don't know the psychology, but it's true. They will discuss the issue, and what the character did, or should do, and can actually be talking about their own problem. It's quite incredible to see. Puppets have the same effect on a lot of kids.

2. It can take out the diversity issue. Animals are animals. No one will say, "There weren't enough tigers in this book!" I don't want to make light of the diversity issues that do exist in picture books, but I also don't believe they should be dealt with in a token way. I also ***also*** believe that diversity in personality is just as, if not more important than race, religion, etc.

3. You can go both ways! They can either be animals as animals dealing with animal things that kids relate to, or animals doing human-like things. Either way, it works ... as long as your story works!

4. Animals, in a children's book, are more malleable. Monsters ***DEFINITELY*** are! You can bonk a monster on the head, drop it from a plane, they basically can't be killed. It's awesome, gives you so much freedom to play, and remember, we are all about play when writing children's books, even serious ones!

HOMEWORK

Now it's time to create animal characters. Usually when I do this with kids we draw a picture of an animal first, but I won't put you through that here. If you ***DO*** want to draw an animal though, scan the QR Code below

or go to:

www.adam-wallace-books.com/free-adam-wallace-drawing-ebooks/

That's where you can download **two how to draw books FOR FREE** that will get you started creating super cool characters you can really start playing around with.

If you don't draw one, pick an animal. We're going to create a character and entire story arc!

First, write down some absolutely true facts about that animal.

For example:

Monkey.

Eats bananas.
Swings in trees.
Has fur.
Lives in the jungle.
Has a tail.

I usually do four or five, but you can do as few or as many as you like.
Go for it, here or in your notebook.

I'll wait.

Dooo dee dooo dee dooooooo.

Keep writing.

Yeah, you're doing great!

Woah, that was a good one!!!

Okay, I'm going to the next page now ...

What we want to do next is really fun, and I started doing this based on books I loved as a kid, written and illustrated by Bill Peet.

The Pinkish, Purplish, Bluish Egg.

Buford the Little Bighorn.

Huge Harold.

All of them feature a creature, oooh that rhymed, and that creature is different to the rest of his herd/pack/council/flock/whatever.

So Huge Harold is a rabbit, but he's huge!

Zeke was hatched by a bird but is actually a griffin.

Buford is a mountain goat, but instead of long legs and horns that curl around his head, Buford has short legs and massssssive horns that go right past his feet.

So then, what we want is all the monkeys to have the traits we wrote on the previous page, but ***OUR*** monkey will be different. So give it character traits or situations that are the opposite or totally different to the facts, as many as you like!

All the monkeys eat bananas, but our monkey is:

Scared of bananas!
Or allergic to bananas.
Or hates the color yellow.

All the monkeys swing in trees, but our monkey:

Is afraid of heights.
Or has no fingers to grip the branches.
Or wants to swing on a human swing in a playground.

All the monkeys have fur, but our monkey:

Has spikes instead of fur.
Or has toenails instead of fur.
Or has flames instead of fur!
Or is bald!

And so on and so on, you get the idea. The more the better, as always!

Now go for it, write down your differences and have fun!

It's also great to think about how the other animals would react to these differences, and in fact that makes these books so special.

Buford holds up the other mountain goats, he's always stumbling and they have to help him so they get annoyed with him.

This leads to the low points.

Buford has to leave the rest of the goats. He's on his own, it's snowing, he's lost and scared, and it's all the fault of these stupid horns!

He hates them and doesn't want them anymore!

Then hunters see him and want to kill him for his horns! **OH NO! It's getting worse!**

He runs away, but stumbles and tumbles down the hillside! It's all over buuuuuut ... he lands in the snow and because his horns are so long, he lands with his feet on his horns and skis away!

Then he becomes a downhill skiing sensation and everyone loves him! So what ***was*** the worst thing in the world (*his horns being too big*) becomes the ***best*** thing in the world!

Do this with your examples. Take your opposites and write out how they could become a great thing at the end of your story!

For example:

Our monkey is afraid of heights, so builds a little house on the ground. Suddenly, all the trees are chopped down, and the other monkeys don't know what to do ... but our monkey does!

He helps them set up a new monkey village on the ground!

Have a go, and as always, play, and as always write down whatever thoughts come to mind!

And finally, before we move on, get into your notebook and write a story from your idea generating! You have a character, the sad but potentially hopeful start, then things go from bad to worse before they become amazing at the end!

Have fun with it, even if it's a serious story. This is practice, and **practice writing is play writing.** There is no write or wrong. Try and keep it picture bookish length, but don't be locked in to that either.

See what comes out. Do it in any style, rhyming, non-rhyming, any age group, whatever you want.

And most of all, ***MOST*** of all, have **FUN!**

SECTION 4

idea

27 PICTURE BOOK IDEAS YOU CAN STEAL AND USE!

HeeeeeRe We GO!

The following are pure stream of consciousness ideas that you are welcome to steal, I mean use! Use them as writing prompts, use them to write a story you will submit for publication, or something in between!

It would actually be hilarious if publishers received 197 submissions all with the same title!!!

So see if they spark something. Maybe some will, or maybe one idea will merge with another idea, or maybe an idea will spark something totally new!

PICTURE BOOK TITLES

Johnny's Banana

Seven ways to trick a sister

What was that?

I know something you don't know

Manny's Many Moods

I got a mug for Christmas

OW! That was hot!

But I don't WANT to eat it! (*I see a series here! But I don't CARE if it's good for me! But it tastes BAD!*)

This prickles, that tickles.

HOMEWORK

If one of those titles felt like it gave you a little spark, start writing a story based on that title.

Whether you do that or not, write down as many new picture book titles as you can! Don't worry about whether they are good or bad or something you feel like you would even write about.

JUST WRITE THEM!

The best ideas will surprise you ... which reminds me of the amazing story of how the **Just Do It** slogan came about!

The story goes that it was inspired by the last words of a man facing execution. They asked him for his last words. He said, "Let's do it." And the rest is history.

(*Seriously! Google "How did Just Do It come about" It's fascinating!*)

Okay. Picture book titles. 

CHARACTERS

(****I might say boy or girl or child or monster or dog, but the character can be anything!****)

A lion who dreams of a sea-change (*or ski-change/ city-change/etc etc*)

A monster whose only goal is to steal every single cockatoo egg in the world.

A child who sees her baby brother as an art canvas.

A monster that can't control its temper.

A monkey that is allergic to bananas.

An ant that is terrified of magnifying glasses ... and a boy with a magnifying glass.

A boy with Tourette Syndrome who can't stop his outbursts, and the librarian who saves him.

Triplets. 11 years old. One shy. One smart. One tough. All pickpockets!

A puppy with the cutest eyes ... who's a bully!

HOMEWORK

Yep, you guessed it ... your turn! I know we've done some character work already, but here is the most important lesson in picture books, nay, in writing in general.

YOU CAN NEVER DO TOO MUCH!!!

EVER!

YOU CAN NEVER WRITE TOO MANY STORIES OR BRAINSTORM TOO MANY IDEAS.

EVER!!!!!!!!

So choose one or more of those character ideas and brainstorm or write a story about it!

Then, once you've done that, create your own characters. Write down every idea of a **new character** that flows out of your brain, good, bad or ugly! Put it all down then sift through for the gold!

And if you think up a character you ***reallly*** love, take that energy and brainstorm and write and play and ***BAM!*** You may have the first draft of the next bestseller!

PICTURE BOOK FIRST LINES/ STANZAS/STORY STARTERS!

Here are 8 story starters you can use to kickstart a story ... but don't feel you have to use them exactly! If your brain tangents somewhere else from these, ***GO FOR IT!!!*** Whatever comes out and is written right now is right!

Write fast, edit slow ... which is a PG variation on Peter de Vries' "Write drunk, edit sober" quote haha!

1. A puppy in Paris with a passion for pastry,
Loved eating biscuits and cakes.
But this puppy in Paris with a passion for pastry,
Was about to make many mistakes.

2. Lottie's room was filled with hats of all shapes, styles and colors. And, on the inside of every single hat, Lottie had written: *I LOVE YOU, GRANDPA.*

3. Why was it there? And where had it come from? No one knew ... except for Taylor.

4. If there was one thing Angus knew, it was that he didn't know anything ... hang on a minute ...

5. A hippo eating cream-filled buns,
Decided that she'd count by ones. (*Then some pages/scenes/somethings of counting by ones*)

A lion who'd escaped from zoos,
Decided that he'd count by twos.

A monkey swinging through the trees,
Decided that he'd count by threes.

6. Sasha never cleaned her room, and with good reason. The mess kept the ghosts in check.

7. "Mum would be ***SO*** angry if she saw me," Harry thought, skating along with a tortoise on his back. Harry thought it was dumb that hippos and tortoises couldn't be friends. It had always been that way, ever since the great pond battle of 1432. But, Harry thought, it's ***DUMB!***

8. Slowly, slowly, ever so slowly, the giant snails slid over the roof of the house.

A PICTURE BOOK TEMPLATE FOR YOU!

This one is a fully-fledged story outline. Again, totally just an idea and suggestions. Use bits of it, or all of it, or none of it. Aim it at a younger or older audience. Different illustration style thoughts. It's yours to do with as you wish!

TITLE: ALDO THE INVENTOR
ILLUSTRATED IN THE STYLE OF:
James Foley
TARGET AGE GROUP: 4-8 years old

CONCEPT: Aldo is an inventor ... just not a very good one! And yes, this is something we have seen before, so how can we make it different?

Aldo's inventions are designed to be loving and make people feel good. Things that give hugs, or massages, or are for fun, but they actually cause chaos, mess, breakages, embarrassment to his family. One even makes his mum lose her job!

Aldo has had enough. He is giving up. He decides to throw all the inventions out the next morning.

But, that night, a burglar breaks into the family home. On the way out, he sees Aldo's inventions and decides that he would like a nice face massage (*or your variation*).

Because it malfunctions, the face massager (*or your variation*) beats him up. He then staggers from one invention to the next, going from bad to worse for the burglar, until he sees one last invention and decides yes, he would like a hug (*or your variation*).

So he goes into the hug machine (*or your variation*) which malfunctions and traps him and keeps him there till the morning when the family see him and call the police.

Who call the media.

And a very big security company pays Aldo a ***LOT*** of money for his inventions!

Aldo's inventions become famous and they ***always*** work ... just not in the way they were supposed to!

THEMES: "Just because something doesn't do what you planned it to do, doesn't mean it is useless." ~ Thomas Edison.

Good intentions can make magic happen.

Be flexible! Be prepared to get to where you want by a different path.

Don't be a burglar!!!

If we want to make the world a better place, we ***will*** find a way!

Don't look at the problem, look past the problem at the solution!

HOMEWORK

So many ideas! Including the ones ***you*** did previously, and my suggestions, and the character things, and the storyboarding and everything else ... **we now have 75 gazillion ideas for stories!**

And people say it's hard to come up with ideas for a story! To them I say ***HA!***

I know we haven't looked at structure, rhyme, non-rhyme, anything like that yet (***that's all coming!***), but for wherever you are now, whatever you feel in your heart about writing picture books, whatever is ready to come out ... choose one of the things we've created, or a mixture of a couple of things, and **write a picture book!**

Word length isn't crucial, especially in a first draft, but it won't hurt to have a word length in mind to aim for. Doesn't matter if you hit it or not, just have it in mind. 500 words is a standard one, so that can be a good start, but it's up to you.

Outside of that, whatever you want to write and however you want to write it is perfect! We will come back to this story, after we have done the other sections, and work on it some more, tightening it up.

But now it's time for you to have **FUN!!!!!**

CREATE!!!

GO!

NOWWWWW!!!

SECTION 5

TO RHYME OR NOT TO RHYME ...

IT'S RHYME TIME!

Rhyming picture books. We all know them. We pretty much all love them. They are crucial in helping kids learn to read. They have a sing-song quality that makes them fun to read to children.

SO WHY ARE WE **ALWAYS** TOLD THAT PUBLISHERS DON'T WANT SUBMISSIONS IN RHYME???

Honestly, I don't totally know, but here are rumors that have passed my way on the grapevine.

1. PUBLISHERS GET A LOT OF STORIES IN RHYME THAT ARE BADLY WRITTEN.

This is a big one, and totally understandable. If you are reading bad rhyme over and over again, you really don't want to read any more of it! I'll look deeper into what bad rhyme is when I talk about how to write good rhyme! If you know what's good, you know what's bad, and vice versa.

I spoke to one publisher who said she gives a story three stanzas. If the rhyme doesn't hit in those, she's out.

2. PUBLISHERS GET A LOT OF STORIES IN RHYME THAT ARE BADLY WRITTEN.

I can't emphasize this one enough. If you are going to write in rhyme, write and test and edit and write and test and edit and read it out loud and get others to read it out loud and get that rhyme amazing! But that is also just the start. Don't get so lost in the rhyme that you lose the story. Story is still key to a great book, no matter how well it rhymes.

3. I THINK THAT'S ALL.

Look, there may be more reasons, and I'm sure if you Google it you will find some, but in the end, it doesn't matter. Find publishers who say rhyming stories are okay to send in, and then send them in ... after you have worked on your craft and on that story till it bleeds ... okay, maybe not that much, but you get the idea!

You have to stand out from the bad rhyme! How? Well, there are some tips coming, my friend. There are some tips coming!

First though, let's do a little work at home.

HOMEWORK

Read some rhyming books that have been published. **Read them to yourself and out loud.** See if there is a difference in how you read it. Read some super popular ones (*Dr Seuss, Aaron Blabey and Julia Donaldson*) as well as some less popular ones. See if there's a difference.

Is it good rhyme? Why? Not so good? Why?

Do they lose the story in striving for the rhyme?

Write down the title, if you think it's good or bad rhyme, a good or bad story, and why. You'll start to get a feel for what rhyming styles, conventions and rhythms work best (*for you!*). Once you know that, writing rhyme becomes so much easier.

TIPS FOR WRITING GOOD RHYMING STORIES.

1. IT DOESN'T HAVE TO HAVE THE SAME NUMBER OF SYLLABLES IN EVERY LINE!

This is one area lots of people get stuck. They think if every line has 11 syllables, or whatever number, the rhyme will read perfectly. Unfortunately, this isn't true.

Say "however" and "animal" out loud. They both have three syllables, but I definitely say animal faster and with emphasis on the **mal** whereas I say however with the emphasis on the **ev**. That emphasis affects the rhythm. Try this with other words that have the same number of syllables and see if you notice a difference.

Or "anyway" and "I went to." Both three syllables but can be said in a number of ways.

2. FORCE PEOPLE TO READ IT YOUR WAY

This is ***HUUUUUGE!*** This is also an area where singers have a massive advantage over picture book authors. Singers ***tell*** people how their song goes, because of how they sing it.

They can fix a poor rhythm simply by holding a note longer!

They can pause between words or lines, have music breaks, put emphasis where they want, and even not do perfect rhymes.

With a rhyming picture book, people read them however ***THEY*** want to! You may think it has a perfect rhythm when you read it, but someone else may read it quite differently.

The easiest way to test this is to read it out loud and see where you put the emphasis and how that affects the rhythm, then **force people to read it how you do!**

For example, read the following couplet out the three different ways (*this is from a story I have written and submitted ... we'll see if it's good rhyme haha!*).

There's no overacting otter, only an overacting you,
We do not have penguins puffing pipes! How could that be true?

There's no overacting otter, only an overacting ***you***,
We do ***not*** have penguins puffing pipes! How could ***that*** be true?

There's no overacting ***otter***, only an ***overacting*** you,
We do not have penguins puffing pipes! ***How*** could that be true?

Did you read them differently?

Did the pace you read them at change?

Did you put emphasis on words that weren't emphasized, ***because*** of the emphasized words?

Did one way work better than the others?

These are all things to think about when writing rhyme. You can play with length and syllables by changing the emphasis. The other trick is punctuation! Making people pause is awesome!

If you're seeing things like ratfish reading to relax,
Here's my advice … ***lay off the snacks!***

Commas, and ... are really crucial in writing rhyme, and can make all the difference in how a story is read.

Remember, you won't be there when most people are reading it so if you want it read a certain way, make it happen!

This is where Dr Seuss is a genius. I try and read his lines wrong, putting emphasis in all sorts of places ... ***AND IT STILL WORKS!***

Genius.

I don't know how he does it, and I guess that's why his books have stood the test of time ... in terms of the rhyme.

Other things have come up about Dr Seuss books in recent times, but that is a whole other story. In fact, that is a whole other ***BOOK!***

For now, let's focus on rhyme, and ways to get people reading in the rhythm you want.

To do that, you can even use ... **PAGE TURNS!!!**

I really wish that had happened on a page turn.

Anyway. Moving on. For example ...

When the weather's nice, I ride my bike,
I hope my bike won't hit a spike.
I ride round all my favorite spots,
I ride through puddles …

(*Page turn, so long pause!*)

And now I'm covered in dots!

The page turn forces the reader to read it how I want, and builds the suspense! This is a super fun way to force pauses.

3. READ YOUR WORK OUT LOUD

Speaking of crucial things, reading something in your head and reading it out loud are two totally different experiences! I know, sounds weird, but trust me.

When you read your work out loud, especially with rhyme, but even prose, suddenly you stumble over sentences you didn't before.

You notice typos.

The rhythm of the stanza before suddenly affects the rhythm of the stanza you're reading (*this is a big one!*).

It's amazing how much this helps you refine your rhyme.

And remember this ... picture books will most often be read aloud to children, by parents or teachers. This means you want to make it the easiest and most interesting out-loud read ever.

The punctuation and emphasis tips help this, for sure, but practicing reading it out loud will help more. Pretend you're reading it to kids. When you do this, you tend to read slower. If a rhyming picture book is on an A4 sheet of paper, readers read as if it's a race!

Read it as if you are reading to children, and as if it's a book, with page turns, and everything changes. Then stop pretending and ***actually*** read it to kids. See if you actually ***do*** read it differently.

4. HAVE OTHER PEOPLE READ YOUR WORK OUT LOUD!

As, or even more important, get lots of ***other*** people to read it out loud. This is crucial ***AND NERVE-WRACKING!***

But ***CRUCIAL!***

Again, you may think you have written it to be read a

certain way, but suddenly people are pausing where they aren't meant to, or putting the emphasis on the wrong word. This is incredibly frustrating but also incredibly helpful.

If you get a few different people to read it out loud, without them hearing the other readings, and they all stumble at the same points, you have some work to do on those points.

5. WRITE HOW YOU TALK

This seems like dumb advice, right? ***We don't talk in rhyme, Adam! Think about it!***

Well, speak for yourself!!!

So many people, like, ***SOOOOO*** many people, write rhyme ***unnaturally***. This makes it feel forced, and usually happens when they consider the rhyme itself to be the most important thing.

The most common mistake is to put words in a different order to how you would naturally say them.

For example:

The bird kept singing, it just wouldn't quit,
As up in its nest, in the tree, it did sit.

I mean, that has so many problems haha! The rhythm is actually okay, but it is ***SO*** unnatural!

In the tree it did sit?

Come on! No one would actually speak like that. It sat in the tree! Write how you talk!

How about:

The bird kept singing, it wasn't the best,
As it sat at the top of the tree in its nest.

I mean, that isn't great either, but at least it sounds a bit more natural! Here's another example:

I went to the shops to get something to eat,
And guess who, on the way, did I meet?

You can see it is easy to get caught up in the rhyme and rhythm. But even if they work, it doesn't mean it's an easy or pleasant story to read.

Have a go at rewriting that last one to make it more natural, but keep the same story.

So it's about someone walking down the street and they want you to guess who they met. Try a few different things. Change the order of the words.

I went to get something to eat at the shop.
Then saw a person who made me stop.

Or you could even totally rewrite it but keep the concept.

I was on my way to the shops, and guess what?
I bumped into Scott ... ***I BUMPED INTO SCOTT!***

6. TRUST YOUR INSTINCTS

You ***know*** what you like in a rhyme. Trust ***that!***

Don't worry about rules and meters and iambic pentameters or Seuss or Shakespeare ... write how it sounds good to you ... **BUT BE HONEST!**

And play with the rules. Learn them, learn them all, then play with them.

For example, from my book Mac O'Beasty:

A meal which was never far away,
For Mac liked to eat at least nine meals a day,
He never cooked his own food, he got take-away,
From the vendors passing by.

Those vendors passed regularly by Mac's plot,
He was easily the best customer they'd got,
In fact, Mac O'Beasty ate such a lot,
The salesman could buy nice houses, put their kids through private school, drive fancy cars and boats, and take nice holidays to exotic locations.

Lead people one way, then surprise them by going in another, and it will have great impact. It isn't something you want to do too often, and I only did this once in this book, but it can work really well!

7. BE CONSISTENT

The flipside of that is being consistent. This really helps people get into the rhythm of your rhyme.

Of course, it can be a real style choice to do a different rhyming type each stanza, but you have to totally nail it.

If you're consistent in your rhythm, it makes it so much easier for other people to read out loud.

For example:

When the moon is full on a snowy night,
Something magical happens when the time is right.
It's not an old silk hat that brings me to life,
But the enchanted snow star shining down at midnight.

I don't thumpity-thump or give warm hugs-
That's for my friends to do.
These clever kids will try to trap me,
But who will catch me ... you?

As you can see, it is a totally different style from the first to second stanza, and then the second stanza rhythm continues for the rest of the book. It's an okay thing to try, I just think it makes it a little tricker to get into the rhythm.

In saying that, one of my books, The Negatees, has a different style every stanza hahaha!

It totally breaks the rules for rhyming and length ... but I love it because it's consistently inconsistent. And I worked every single stanza to within an inch of its life, so that no matter what came before, it was obvious how that stanza was going to go.

Here's a little sample.

In the land of the smelly trees,
Amongst the flies, the ticks and the fleas,
Lived a creature called The Negatees,
And he lived a sorry life.

The Negatees was a negative fellow,
Bright yellow,
Ate jello,
But a negative fellow.

He had successes, this is true,
Of course he did, we all do.
The Negatees though, in his negative way,
Thought that the bad things would outweigh,
The good, by a factor of two.

One day he went down to the shops to buy,
Something for dinner that night.
Perhaps three lizards, and the head of a fly,
And an eye poked out in a fight.

He mumbled and grumbled the whole way there,
'I bet the lizards are covered in hair.
The eye probably won't have a pupil in there,
My life's just really not fair.'

Okay, I wrote a little more there than I had planned, but I was getting into it, okay?????

As Steve Martin says, “Well excuuuuuuuuuuse meeeeeeee!”

Hahaha I love when he does that.

Anyway, how did you go reading it? Did you read it to yourself or out loud? Did you stumble at certain points or find it easy to read, despite the constant changes in rhythm?

It was a real risk to do a book like this, but it was also ***SO*** much fun, and exciting to take on the challenge.

It was also a really long picture book, so again broke all the rules, and I was so grateful to find a publisher prepared to take that risk,and with amazing illustrations by Heath McKenzie, it did really well.

Again, know the rules so you can break them, but also be prepared that others, including publishers and readers, may not want to break those rules with you.

8. READ, READ, READ AND FIND DIFFERENT STYLES

The more rhyme you read, the more you discover what you like, and what style suits you.

The two main styles I use are rhyming couplets, and whatever the other one is called hahaha, where the second and fourth lines in a stanza rhyme.

So couplets like this from ***Better Out Than In*** ...

The week had begun, things weren't looking good,
Because you weren't feeling as well as you should.
Your tummy was swirling around and around,
You felt like hurling all over the ground!

Or this ***from my new Christmas book*** ...

The day before Christmas is a wonderful time,
With magic and joy in the air.
But one Christmas, long ago, before you were born,
The magic? It just wasn't there.

And of course there are many others. From ***Mac O'Beasty*** again ...

A long time ago, in a land far away,
There lived a monster who, I have to say,
Enjoyed just sitting and eating all day,
In his swamp, on a bed of slime.

Or this from ***Merry Christmas, Adam*** ...

Come on, Adam, join my crew,
We're not cows, so we don't moo,
We're not ghosts, we don't say, "BOO!"
We're wolves! We howl! Let's go!
"AHOOOOOOOOOOOOOOOOO!"

OR this from my uncle's wedding ...

There once was a man named Enis,

Oh. Whoops. Better not finish that one!

But you ***CAN*** do limerick style as well! Like this one I showed before, from ***The Negatees*** ...

He had successes, this is true,
Of course he did, we all do.
The Negatees though, in his negative way,
Thought that the bad things would outweigh,
The good, by a factor of two.

Play with rhyme. It's seriously one of the mostest funnest ways to write books for kids, and you have so many options on how to do it.

The more you play with it, the more you will find your voice and your style, and the easier it will be to focus on the story rather than the rhyme. Once you can do that, the rhyme becomes more natural, the story becomes easier to read, and everyone has a better time!

9. A GREAT RESOURCE

The more rhyming words you know, the quicker you can write, which leads to a more natural sounding story. So building a rhyming dictionary in your head is great, but if you get stuck, check out:

www.rhymezone.com

It is amazing!!!! I have it open ***ALL*** the time while I am writing, so I can look up a rhyming word straight away and be right back into the story.

One that was fun was I was looking for an M word that rhymed with lobster, and couldn't think of one. Went on Rhymezone and ... MOBSTER!!! So mobster monkey it was!

Rhymezone is great for experienced or beginner rhymers, and kids too, but beware! As it doesn't censor its rhyming words, swear words can pop up in there as well. So it might be an idea to monitor children when they're using it.

You can also buy rhyming dictionaries, yep, actual books, which can be very, very helpful too!

HOMEWORK

Read rhyming books and write in rhyme and read rhymes out loud ... over and over and over and over and over and over and over again.

Seriously.

Writing in rhyme is one of the areas that working on your craft over and over will lead to massive improvement.

Like, massive!

I have also put a few rhyming examples here that could use some work. Play with them and see if you can get them sounding awesome ... and then, maybe, even write a story! Don't worry about getting it in one go, have a few goes at rewriting each one if you need to.

The first couple are ones we've already looked at.

The bird kept singing, it just wouldn't quit,
As up in its nest, in the tree, it did sit.

I went to the shops to get something to eat,
And guess who, on the way, I did meet?

Have a go at rewriting the following first stanza with the same rhythm the second stanza has! Or vice versa. And even do it so the rhyme is tighter - night, right, life, midnight is close, but grates on me a little.

When the moon is full on a snowy night,
Something magical happens when the time is right.
It's not an old silk hat that brings me to life,
But the enchanted snow star shining down at midnight.

I don't thumpity-thump or give warm hugs-
That's for my friends to do.
These clever kids will try to trap me,
But who will catch me ... you?

Wonderful. Now, your final challenge, should you choose to accept it, is one I do all the time and love doing. Find a story you have already written that **IS NOT** in rhyme.

Rewrite it, but rewrite it as a rhyming story. This can be quite a challenge, but is actually super rewarding.

As an example, this is the start of a prose story a publisher had that I rewrote in rhyme. I was also trying to shorten it for them.

"Oh, my dearest Robin, you are such a special boy," his mum loved to warmly tell her little Robin. "You have such a big heart, you are curious, friendly to everyone and so deeply compassionate. Ever since you were born, I have known that Mother Earth has chosen you as one of her own..."

And then she always described an event that had taken place at the maternity ward when she had pressed him against her chest for the very first time.

"It was a beautiful sunny day, I pulled you closer and suddenly noticed a bushy branch of a large tree in front of my window ...

And so on. When I did it in rhyme ...

When Robin was born, the sky was blue,
It was a wonderfully sunny day.
He slept with his mother, lying on her chest,
On the bed in Ward 8J.

Okay! Your turn! Take one of your prose stories and rewrite it in rhyme. If you ***haven't*** written something in prose, take a picture book someone else has done and rewrite it in rhyme!

And, as always, ***HAVE FUN WITH IT!!!***

SECTION 6

WRITING FOR/ WITH AN ILLUSTRATOR!!!

EVERY PICTURE BOOK HAS 3 STORIES

This is something Leigh Hobbs, picture book legend, says. I may be kind of getting it slightly not exactly word perfect, but basically, in a picture book:

The text tells one story.

The pictures tell another story.

The third story is the one the kids make up in their own mind!

Or he might say the third story is the one the text and pictures tell together, or it's the gap between the text and pictures, I can't remember exactly ... either or any way, it's good!

The pictures don't have to, and in fact ***shouldn't***, be an exact reflection of the text. It's a chance to explore and play and add so much!

So how do we ***write*** to leave space for that gap? Well, you don't need to worry about it so much in a first draft, just get everything in there. But as you edit, it's really important to think about what could be left out, and shown in the pictures.

This gets easier the more you do it, but there are definitely some things to think about.

1. DESCRIPTION

Description is ***DEFINITELY*** one thing that can be eased up on in picture books.

In a story I'm writing at the moment, initially it was like this ...

While the guards were distracted, Eve went to the box,
Tore a corner of wrapping away.
Then she snuck inside, and what she saw,
Filled her heart with dismay.

Although, on the outside, the box was bright,
With colors, patterns and a bow.
Inside was dark, and dank, and cold,
Eve's spirits sunk so low.

That second stanza is lovely and descriptive, and I love the word dank, but **it isn't necessary!** We have the first stanza to introduce the box, and the picture will show her going inside, so that second stanza is unnecessary!

We'll also be able to see from her expression how low her spirits have sunk, and we kinda say that at the end of the first stanza anyway!

BAM! Stanza gone!

You don't need to write how a character has long hair, or whose eyes narrow, or who is shocked. You ***CAN***, but you don't have to if the picture can show it for us.

You can be much more general! Same with place description. **They entered the creepy forest** gives the illustrator ***SO*** much more freedom than **They entered the forest, which was dark, and eyes stared at them from the trees, and the branches on the trees looked like arms, and there was a wolf sitting on the path and ghosts in the shadows!**

Over describing is like writing an instruction guide for your illustrator. They have been hired on this project to bring more out of your words than you could ever have imagined.

So let them do that.

Trust them!

Give them the freedom to play that you had in writing the story.

And all of this isn't to say that you can't write description. Some of the most beautiful books ever made have lovely description. It's about finding the balance between text and pictures.

When you can do that, find that sweet spot, that's where the magic lies.

2. WRITE OPEN, NOT CLOSED

This is similar to the description thing.

The storm closed in is open.

The skies turned grey and the wind howled, knocking over trees and sending people scurrying for shelter is closed. Fine for a novel, not so much for a picture book.

We can show the scurrying people and trees falling in the pictures.

Okay, I'm going to stop rambling on about this. Basically, you don't need to write details! That's the crux of this! ***Write the internal, what the character thinks and feels, show the external in the pictures.***

Give hints, show answers!

Basically, writing open and leaving space gives ***YOU*** room to play!.

Check out this rough from a book I am doing with James Hart! I'm going to rotate it so I can make it as big as possible, it's just that good.

Just a quick heads up, James is a genius. 'Nuff said.

"These cakes look delicious," Charlie cried.
"I can't look away!"

James and I took ***SO*** much delight in taking Leigh's concept to the extreme, creating a **MASSIVE** gap between text and picture.

The joke of the story is that Charlie and his mum walk to school, but are always looking at something and never notice the chaos going on behind them. And in that chaos, James has about 5 storylines going on!

This lets the kids fill in gaps and notice everything else. Also, if we had to write exactly what was going on in this picture, **it would be a million words!**

It's like silence on a stage. Don't be scared to leave silence in your text ... a great illustrator will not only fill the silence, but make it ear-splitting!

Basically, in an educational reader, the picture can be exactly what the text says, as that helps with kids learning to read. It's also kinda boring.

In a fiction picture book, it is wonderful if the picture can give more, add more to the text.

HOMEWORK

For the following two pictures/scenes, have a go at **A)** writing text that fits exactly what is going on, and **B)** writing text that leaves a gap.

See which one strikes you as more interesting. I won't tell you what I wrote in the book either!

Go on. Write it in your notebook, and see what you come up with.

Now read some of your favorite picture books you chose earlier. See if you can find the gaps, the missing bits that could have been written, but weren't.

Then try and rewrite some pages fully, as if there was no gap, and see how it flows ... if it flows at all!

SECTION 7

USING MOVIE STRUCTURES FOR PICTURE BOOKS!

MOVIES? BUT THEY'RE SO LONG!

They sure are! But if we look outside the world of picture books for inspiration, suddenly we can have much fuller stories, and we can have tighter structures!

And, if you think about it, a picture book is to a movie like a T-rex is to a chicken! The closest relative!

And we can scale a picture book to a standard movie structure! Many books on screenwriting break a screenplay into pages ... and the theory is a page a minute. So scale that!

If a 100 page screenplay is 100 minutes, and something should happen by page 10, that's 10% into the story. Easy! That's two or three pages into our picture book.

There's an important moment at Page 25 of a movie? Well now, that's 25% through the picture book which is seven or eight pages in! And so on!

There's so much more we can learn from movies too. As ***Robert Ben Garant and Thomas Lennon*** say in their **AMAZING** book, **Writing movies for ~~FUN AND~~ PROFIT (*EXCELLENT* book!)**, there is a simple structure to great movies.

ACT 1: Put a likeable guy up a tree.
ACT 2: Throw rocks at him.
ACT 3: Get him down.

Another director, **Irving Thalberg**, who did Marx Brothers movies among others, said a good movie is like a game of American Football. The home team is driven back again and again and again, and then, with no time left on the clock, they do an amazing run down the field for a touchdown and the win.

In **Save the Cat**, ***Blake Snyder*** talks about how even an unlikeable hero needs a moment at the start that shows something good about them, that they can change, that makes us root for them to do so.

Think about that if you have a potentially unlikeable character you want to change. What can they do early on for us to want them to change, to succeed?

The Hero's Journey, from ***Joseph Campbell***, has amazing moments that are used in movies that we can totally use in our picture books! An inciting incident, the hero refusing to take the call to action then being forced to, a mentor and so on.

I found **The Hero's Journey** a tough book to get through, but there are great summaries on the internet that break it down. It's worth checking out.

The Dan Harmon Story Circle is similar and is excellent as well, and can apply to the story as a whole, and/or the individual characters.

Kurt Vonnegut does an ***INCREDIBLE*** talk on the shape of stories. Scan the QR code to check it out.

This is brilliant, and something I use all the time, in picture books and longer stories as well.

Robert McKee talks about needing a positive and a negative turning point in each scene of a movie. We can build this into our picture books too! Each spread can have a high and a low, or can have that every few pages.

And remember, a positive for our protagonist is a negative for their nemesis!

We can use all these ideas in our picture books, or as inspiration for them! Fo sho! And I'm going to show you how right now!

On the next page.

Soon.

Almost, be patient.

Okay, turn the page and check it out!

The Likeable Character Structure

Put a likeable character up a tree.

Throw rocks at him.

Get him down.

It's such a simple structure! We have a character that is likeable, so the reader will relate to them or at least want them to succeed (*Yep, it works for likeable characters as well as unlikeable characters*).

We throw obstacles at them, preferably ones that grow and escalate as the story goes along. We want the last obstacle to be the biggest, so we are desperate for our character to win.

Then, at the end, they win, and everyone's satisfied!

Right? **Right!**

How can we apply this to picture book ideas?

Perhaps you have a nice kid who is being bullied. They could ***literally*** have rocks thrown at them! While they're up a tree! Why not take these things literally and make them into a story?

How about a kid who is naughty but charming? Likeable doesn't have to mean sweet and nice.

We all know these kids. Sometimes the naughty kids are not only the most memorable, but the most likeable in a weird way. Ask any teacher! They are more likely to remember the cheeky kids than the ones who fly under the radar.

So use this to your advantage. Make your character likeable, and the reader will want them to succeed.

THE SPORTS GAME STRUCTURE

Oh boy, how we love an underdog in movies and books, and especially in sports movies!

Rocky 1 through Rocky 7!

Rudy, Heart of a hero!

The Replacements!

Then there are the inspirational teacher movies, getting kids no one believes in to rise above their circumstances and past!

Stand and Deliver!

Freedom Writers!

Coach Carter (*This is sports* ***AND*** *inspirational teacher* ***AND*** *awesome***)**

Dangerous Minds!

The list goes on. True stories get us too, even in talent shows on TV. Susan Boyle, anyone? Remember her? And there have been many like her since, where the audience scoffs and laughs at first, then is blown away.

Underdogs get us cheering and excited and knowing they might win but it seems impossible and we can feel the odds are so against them there's no way they can possibly do it but oh my God they did do it ***WOOOOOOOOO!!!***

Stack the odds against your character. And make it ***REALLY*** hard. Actually, make it seemingly impossible for them to reach their goal. Throw everything at them so the win is more satisfying!

This is the Rocky theory, or the Irving Thalberg one I mentioned as well. Push them back, hold them down, block them out, and then, when they come through, oh boy it makes your heart sing!

And you can play with this as well. Maybe they don't reach the goal they were after, but gain something much more. They don't win the final game but find something within themselves they didn't know they had.

Play with this. See what comes out. See if you feel inspired while writing one of these. If you do, chances are the reader will as well!

SAVING THE CAT

Maybe our naughty character has a puppy they love dearly. In lots of movies, the gangsta kids are sweet to their sick mother, or their little siblings. Maybe the bully looks after pigeons, a la Mike Tyson.

It can be anything, but we need something to put out there to give the reader hope that change is a-comin'!

THE HERO'S JOURNEY

This is a little harder to fit into a picture book, but it can definitely be done.

The inciting incident takes out character out of their normal world, a mentor guides them (*but in the end it* ***MUST*** *be the main character that saves the day, and it can't just be by luck*), the moment when all seems lost is crucial, and then the final victory and/or the change in the character.

Peter Carnavas is amazing at the all is lost moment, often using a beautiful wordless spread to really hammer it home. Check out his books!

Think of all your favorite movies. That moment when it seems like there's no way the main character or characters can win, how do you feel? I feel like lurching out of my seat to help them! Imagine kids feeling that emotion from a book!

THE SHAPE OF STORIES

The Kurt Vonnegut thing. I have this as a go to ***SO*** often. We want, nay, we ***need*** positives and negatives through a story. Even if the character is being pushed back again and again, there must be little wins, little glimmers of hope, little clues as to what's coming.

If it's all downhill then flies up, it seems to come out of the blue. We need to see the character, the values, the belief in our hero, and along the way let ***THEM*** see the glimmer of hope as much as we do!

But a flat graph sucks too. If everything just trots along at the same level of good or bad, that would be a hella boring story. Curves are good, and even angled lines with little spikes work nicely!

A picture book can have a simple or a complex graph, and can be more complex depending on the age group targeted. I like the Vonnegut one.

Kid gets something.

Kid loses it.

Kid gets it again, or gets something much better!

BAM! Picture book!

Positive and Negative Turning Points

This works wonderfully in movies, especially if you have something that ***seems*** positive, but turns out to be negative. This also fits in well with Dan Harmon's story circle, where he inserts a false victory or loss.

What's fun to write and watch is also when it ***seems*** positive (*or negative*) to the main character, but ***we*** know it is actually a negative (*or positive!*)!

The fun of picture books is we can totally play with this, and it goes back to the text and pictures telling different stories. Have the text be positive, but drop something in the picture that shows it isn't, or that hints at a path that will be negative.

Or vice versa ... remember, the character can't read what we write, or always see what we draw (***"It's behind you!"***), so we can put in anything we like, really mess with the character hahaha!

YOUR FAVORITE MOVIE THEMES

This idea and exercise was given to me by Michael Wagner (*legend of Australian Children's books*), who got it from somewhere else. The idea is you look at your top 5 or 10 favorite movies, and see if there is a common theme (*Mine, scarily, is revenge! But also the underdog coming through. Michael's is family*).

This then, is a theme you can use when writing! It may be family, or love, or friendship, or revenge, or whatever. Weave it into your stories, and you will find the writing tends to flow much easier because it excites you as you write it.

And then, once that is done, I shall overcome the odds and revenge shall be mine ***mwawhahahahahahahahaha!!!***

*****NOTE: Theme isn't genre! You may have 5 favorite horror movies ... but the theme may be different in all of those movies! It could be friends sticking together, or regret for past actions, or just plain old silly fun.**

Dig into that, look deeper than the genre, and you will find the themes you can then apply to *ANY* genre!

HOMEWORK

So they are tips we can take from movies and apply to our picture books ... so let's apply them!

First, let's do that theme thing. Write down your top 5 or 10 movies and see if a certain theme pops up regularly.

Then, taking one of the ideas from earlier in this book, yours or mine, write a story based around your theme.

You can just write it, or you can think about some of the structural movie tips we have looked at too - positive and negative turning points, Hero's Journey, whatever struck a chord with you.

Follow the energy.

Sounds tricky, but once you have the structure and theme (*and we've done characters and other bits earlier as well!*), now you have the bones, all you gotta do is add the blood and guts!

Then, take a nap or watch an awesome movie!

SECTION 8

FLIP THE SCRIPT WITH PAGE TURNS

GIVING CAUSE FOR PAUSE

As we looked at in the **forcing people to read how you want them to** part of the book, we can also use the layout to give people a breather, or to build anticipation, or to accentuate a moment, or just to make the book more awesome.

The best way I know to do this, and there are others but this is my favorite, is via page turns.

PAGE TURNS

OH HOW I LOVE YOU, PAGE TURNS!!!!!

I realized the awesomeness of page turns when I illustrated my first book. Before that, I would write a story straight out, send it in, then marvel at the way it came out.

I also can't visualize, so I never really even saw the story as a book, or thought about how it would look. This, I now realize, was missing out on a huge advantage in writing a more awesome story.

Once I was illustrating as well, it suddenly clicked that I could set up a joke at the end of a right hand page ...

AND THEN THE PAGE TURN WOULD REVEAL AN ILLUSTRATION OR LINE THAT WAS THE PUNCHLINE!

It's ***SO*** fun!

It can also be used to trick the reader, as they are turning blind. There are so many options.

You can give them what they expect, which is especially great with young kids. But you can play with that too! Give them what they expect for a bit, then flip it!

You can do this by building their expectations in one direction and take them in another. This builds tension, and you can build it and build it ... and then release when the page turn isn't what they thought!

It also works great with jokes and gives you options for a fun twist! It builds anticipation, it's awesome!

In the example I gave earlier, the lead up is always the same to the page turn ...

When the weather's nice, I ride my bike,
I hope I don't ride over a spike.
I ride round all my favorite spots,
I ride through puddles and … (*Page turn, so a long pause!*)

Now I'm covered in dots!

This happens numerous times, the ***Now I'm*** line rhyming with the previous page's last line, until around the middle of the book, when you get this ...

I ride over jumps, I get some air,
The wind is flying through my hair!
I jump so high it's like I'm flying,
Then I crash and now I'm ... (***PAGE TURN***)

Acting super tough because Janice is watching.

I also do this in ***There's a Bullant in the Bedroom,*** my equal favorite rhyming story I've ever done. The page turn here was built into the story before the pitch as a crucial element, and was so much fun to play with. It builds for a few stanzas then flips.

A page turn can also skip time! Maybe, in your story, monkeys have been appearing at a steady rate, one or two per page, but what next? Turn the page ... oh man! There are thousands of them!

It's really cool, when you're writing a story, to have page turns in mind. They can be used to massive advantage in helping you "see" the story!

It's also an advantage if, I mean, **when** you submit, because it shows you've thought about page turns, and how they can make your amazing story even better!

HOMEWORK

Read some picture books and see if and how they use page turns. I have found that not a lot of books use them to advantage, so considering this can really put you ahead of the field.

In such a crowded market, we have to look for ways to stand out, and excellent use of page turns is one of those ways.

There's a Bullant in the Bedroom, as I said, is one I used page turns in to build and break expectations. And it was ***SO*** fun to do that!

I think ***Stuck*** does it best of all, and this is a totally unbiased opinion as it is just about my favorite picture book of all time!

Do NOT Open This Book plays on page turns really well, too. Don't turn the page! ***AAAGGGHHH***, you turned the page! Again, it's building expectation, and the reaction from kids shows how well it works.

Page turns and building expectation is also amazing for readalouds. It enables you to get the kids to guess what's coming next. They will say the most hilarious things, and get so excited when they are right. It also brings forth squeals when there's a twist.

Okay, more work for you to do. For one of the stories you wrote before, or one you've written previously, have a read through and see if there are any points at which you may be able to employ the awesomeness of a page turn.

Sometimes it can be as simple as a scene change, from light to dark, as we explored when looking at the stanza to leave out of my Christmas story.

SECTION 9

THE STRUCTURE SUPER SUCCESSFUL BOOKS USE!!!

WHAT IS THIS MAGICAL STRUCTURE?

Wouldn't you like to know? Yeah, I guess you would, that's why we're here!

This is actually so cool, and I was so excited when I discovered it. It isn't in **all** successful picture books, of course, but ***it is in some of the biggest!***

Basically, it's a story that's more a series of events. Here's how it works, and it's especially good for rhyming stories (*but doesn't have to be in rhyme ... see* **STUCK** and **Do NOT Open This Book!**).

ACT 1

You start off with an **introductory stanza or three** (*Or a few spreads for non-rhyming*) which shows us the main character(s) and the gist of the story (*going on a holiday, leprechaun is in town, kids want to catch him, whatever*).

In the How to Catch series, it's introducing the creature the kids are going to try and catch, and why. It does this even if it's in first or second person.

ACT 2

The **next nine or ten stanzas/spreads** (*20 pages*) are a series of events, often funny, always escalating, either in scale, or in being harder and harder for the main character to reach their intention, or both.

In the How to Catch books, the brief was to make the traps bigger and bigger as we went along, which was ***SO MUCH FUN*** to write and then to see them brought to life by the amazing illustrator, Andy Elkerton.

ACT 3

In **the last couple of stanzas/spreads**, a goal is reached and we sum it all up.

In saying that, in the How to Catch books, the goal of the kids trying to catch the creature is ***NEVER*** reached. However, the goal of the creature trying to get away ***IS*** reached every time!

14 stanzas. A spread per stanza, leaving lots of space for fun in the illustrations.

This gives you 28 pages of text for a 32 page picture book, and generally around 450-500 words ... which is **perfect for submitting!**

It's also perfect for kids as the story builds, trying to guess what's coming next as the story escalates, but also trying to work out how the character will 'win'.

Obviously page counts and word counts can be played with, but the general idea of this works really well **every ... single ... time!**

BOOKS THAT USE THIS STRUCTURE

So what are some books that use this structure?

Pig the Pug by **Aaron Blabey** is a ***HUGELY*** successful (*and totally awesome*) series that follows this structure. In fact, it was **Pig the Tourist** that opened my eyes to it.

In this series of books, it's Christmas, or a trip, or Pig won't share. Then there is a series of Pig doing very, very funny things, usually him being not very nice. In the last couple of stanzas, Pig gets his just desserts in a painful way!

Kids love the familiarity, even if they don't necessarily realize the structure is the same in the books. **There's a theory our brains love things that are 85% familiar and 15% original.**

If it's too familiar, it's boring. If it's too original, it freaks us out. So a solid structure but with different events and antics is perfect!

As mentioned earlier, in my ***How to Catch*** series, each one starts with a couple of stanzas introducing the elf, or leprechaun, or unicorn, and the idea that the kids are going to try and catch them.

Then there are 8 or 9 increasingly crazy traps, ending with the biggest of all. Then the final stanza is the character saying, basically, "Tough luck, kids! I win! Better luck next year!"

This varies a little in later books, as the character may help the kids escape, or win a science comp, etc, but they still always get away.

STUCK, by ***Oliver Jeffers***, is the greatest picture book I have ever read. It starts with the kid playing and his ball gets stuck up the tree. He employs increasingly crazy and beautifully written attempts to get the ball down, but fails every time ... until he doesn't. He plays for a bit, goes to bed, then the twist is he wakes up realizing he's forgotten everything is still up the tree. It's wonderful.

DO NOT OPEN THIS BOOK, written by the hilarious ***Andy Lee***, and illustrated by the amazing ***Heath McKenzie***, also follows this idea really well. The monster says do not open the book, and gets increasingly angry, until the end when he collapses in exasperation!

The Monster at the End of This Book by ***Jon Stone*** does it too!

CHARACTER, INTENTION AND OBSTACLE

As we looked at earlier, it is character, intention and obstacle that drives these stories. When you have a character that really wants something, but put everything you can in its way, the results are glorious and often hilarious! It's getting the person up the tree, throwing rocks at them, and getting them down (*or putting them up another tree haha!*)

It's also so much fun to escalate these obstacles throughout the book. This structure, as much as any, allows you to really use your imagination and play.

The other great thing about using this structure is that it is **ENDLESS!!!!!!!** You are only limited by the situations you can think up. It also means you can really create a series around it.

The ***How to Catch*** books just use a different creature and traps.

Do Not Open This Book has different scenarios of the same idea and is up to ten books at the time of me writing this.

Great character, great structure, great series!

HOMEWORK

Take one of the characters you thought up in a previous homework section, or from the story ideas I gave. Brainstorm on ways you could use the structure we've been talking about with that character.

Certainly from my character ideas, the **lion dreaming of a sea-change** is perfect! Because then it can be city-change, country-change, whatever, and the obstacles would be super fun to put in!

In the first few spreads, the lion dreams of leaving where he lives. Then he ***does*** leave.

We can then go one of a few ways. Obstacles can be put in his way to ***stop him leaving***, so that in every book he never actually leaves.

Orrrr obstacles could be put in his way while he's ***trying to get there***, so he never makes it and always returns to the other lions.

Or he can make it to the new place easily, then obstacles get put in his way when he's there. This will mean he always ends up returning home as **a)** the place he wanted to be isn't as amazing as he'd thought it would be, or **b)** it doesn't suit a lion, or **c)** he realizes his home is actually better than he'd thought.

This would work great with other things too, like a penguin or snowman or anything/anyone dreaming of more!

SECTION 10

3 MORE PICTURE BOOK TEMPLATES YOU CAN STEAL ... I MEAN, USE!

POTENTIAL PICTURE BOOK TEMPLATE NUMBER 1!!!

Remember that this, and the following ideas, are **just templates**. Use them, twist them, play with them however you want. Maybe use the title, maybe some of the themes, maybe the whole thing!

TITLE: **TOO MANY CHEFS**
ILLUSTRATED IN THE STYLE OF: James Hart
TARGET AGE GROUP: 4-8 years old

CONCEPT: A restaurant opens, but the owner is really bad at making decisions and telling people no. So he hires ***ALL*** the chefs that applied for the job. It's like a clown car in that kitchen!

In the lead up to the grand opening, the chefs can't work together, get in each others' way, argue over the type of food they should be serving, bump into each other, spill food everywhere, have a massive food fight.

How will they ever work together?

Options: The owner stands up and becomes a leader.

The chefs cause a fire because of their pettiness and stop the place burning down ... as a team. They ***CAN*** work together.

They realize all types of foods can be on the menu.

Or you may write something totally different, whatever pops into your head.

Either way, the opening of the restaurant is a massive success.

A possible last page shows the owner saying he is thinking of opening up a pastry bar as well, and will have a bake-off to see who will be the head pastry person. This leads into Book 2!

THEMES: Teamwork.
Leadership.
Seeing other people's skills.
Not always having to be right.
Learning to say no.
How to open a restaurant.

POTENTIAL PICTURE BOOK TEMPLATE NUMBER 2!!!

TITLE: BEST FRIENDS
ILLUSTRATED IN THE STYLE OF: Nicky Johnston
TARGET AGE GROUP: 4-8 years old

CONCEPT: This utilizes the Romeo and Juliet concept, of two households at war, but love occurs across the families.

Obviously we can't have romantic love ... or suicide/ murder haha! But we can use this (*and many other public domain stories at our disposal!*).

It's The Fox and the Hound as well, a great movie if you haven't seen it.

In my mind, this is aliens from different planets that hate each other and no one hardly even knows why any more. The original thing has been twisted and turned into something that isn't even real.

Two young aliens, one from each planet, meet and hit it off. They sneak off and play at every interval, hiding the fact they are friends, because they know what it will cost, and that it won't be allowed. It's been drilled into them from birth that they must hate each other.

A twist to this is they meet and hit it off and become friends, with no idea they're not meant to, which is what kids do! They often don't care about the stupid stuff adults care about!

Eventually, they are caught out. The parents enforce their will, and one friend is terrible to the other, saying they were tricked/trapped, and saying that all the awful things about aliens from that planet are true.

They do it to save themselves, but the twist is they actually do it to save their friend. The innocent friend has no idea, however, and is shattered. Maybe they are even taken prisoner!

With the planets now on the brink of war, the free friend must go against their family and, potentially, everything they have been taught to believe, to save the friend, and in turn, save the planets.

A good twist would be for them to use what is seen as a weakness and turn it into a strength. "We hated you for such and such, but it actually is good because ..."

THEMES: Friendship.
Racism.
Stereotypes.
Seeing past rumors.
The stupidness of centuries old rivalries.
The strength of love and friendship to overcome dumb traditions and rivalries.

POTENTIAL PICTURE BOOK TEMPLATE NUMBER 3!!!

TITLE: I'M THE BIGGEST OF ALL

ILLUSTRATED IN THE STYLE OF: Dr Seuss

TARGET AGE GROUP: 4-8 years old

CONCEPT: I love this concept! It plays on the idea that there is always someone better and worse off than you. Everything is relative. ***EVERYTHING!*** Sometimes the things we take for granted, or think are our problems, can be other people's greatest dream.

But it also plays on the fact there is ***no such thing*** as hot, or cold, or tall, or anything! They're concepts, constructs! 8 degrees is cold? It might **seem hot to someone** from the South Pole, **but freezing to someone** from the Bahamas!

A child is the tallest in their class, so they're tall ... right? Not if they are in a room full of giants, they're not! Or even adults!

Someone is super strong, and can beat up the other kids ... until a new kid comes to school.

A kid lauds it over everyone else how rich they are, until they move to a new suburb and are the poorest ones there!

A kid is the stinkiest of all, and loves it, but then goes to a Baked Beans Convention and is out-gassed.

And so on, a series of events that lead to the kids being confused. If I'm not the richest/fastest/smelliest/smartest/strongest/etc, then who am I? I was special because I could ***DO*** this better or ***LOOK*** better than anyone, but now I realize that's not always true!

And the beautiful thing is that what makes them special is that they are them! Yep, great English there, but you know what I mean!

I also like the idea that what makes us special (*or the opposite*) isn't what we were born with or into, like looks or money or size, but rather what is inside, ***the things we are by choice rather than chance.***

THEMES: Defining ourselves by looks/stature.
Defining ourselves by our job/talent/etc. If we lose that, who are we?
Competition.
Arrogance.
Seeing past appearances.
Nothing is real it's all in our perception of it.
Self-worth versus self-confidence

I actually got excited about this one and had a play at a first and last stanza in rhyme. Obviously, you can write it however you like, but are also welcome to use these!

FIRST STANZA:

Look at me! I'm the **BIGGEST** of all,
I'm pretty much a giant, I'm so tall.
But when I'm with ***actual*** giants, I start musing,
Now I am the ***smallest*** … this is confusing!

LAST STANZA:

If I'm ***not*** the biggest, if I'm ***not*** always tall,
If I'm ***not*** the stinkiest or fastest of all.
It doesn't matter one bit, because I finally see,
I'm the greatest at one thing, and that's being … ***ME!***

SECTION 11

EDITING YOUR PICTURE BOOK!

Editing a picture book is just like editing any other sort of book ... kinda sorta.

You read through, you look for mistakes, you check the readability, but there's a little bit more as well. Some of this little bit more comes before the illustrations, some comes during the layout, and some comes after all of that!

We have covered some of this in previous sections, but it's always worth revising these things as they can be so important in the finished product being as good as it can possibly be!

Also, if you can do a chunk of this before submitting to a publisher, they will be very impressed that there is potentially less work for them to do.

READ IT OUT LOUD

We talked about this in the rhyming section, as in you and I "we", not the royal "we".

Anyway.

Reading your story out loud is an **INVALUABLE** editing tool. You notice mistakes you don't notice when you read to yourself, as your mind fills in the gaps.

Reading it out loud isn't an iron-clad guarantee you'll get every mistake, but it sure gets a lot of them.

My first book, **Better Out Than In**, was self-published, and I did the editing myself, although I gave it to other people to read as well.

That book of 6 short stories was read hundreds of times!

Then I printed it, showed it to Mum, and on the first page she went, “You made a mistake.”

WHAAAAAAAAAAAAAAAAAAAAAAT?????

I had written you instead of your, and we had all missed it reading it in our heads as we knew it was meant to be your so filled it in!

Read it out loud.

This is not only great for finding mistakes, but also helping with punctuation. Notice where you pause. Haven’t got a comma, full stop or ellipses there? ***PUT ONE IN!***

See where you stumble. See where there seems to be too much writing on a page.

Reading it out loud, over and over again, and not rushing through it, but reading it with purpose and patience, will be the best picture book editing tool you will ever use.

Aside from AI. But that’s another story ...

LISTEN TO OTHER PEOPLE READING IT OUT LOUD!

This is crucial, crucial I say! It's a chance to see if readers stumble, or look confused as they read, where they pause, ***how*** they pause, if they read it how you want them to, all of that!

REMOVE UNNECESSARY WORDS!

This gets easier the more you do it, but picture books are concise, beautiful, tightly written works of art. Don't waffle. Imagining illustrations can be really helpful for this.

If it isn't necessary, or you feel like it needs to get to the point, tighten it! Cut out words you don't need.

This is just as important in prose picture books as rhyming ones. Be short, sharp, to the point ... and let the pictures fill in those descriptive words!

LAY IT OUT LIKE IT'S A BOOK!

Yep, just write Page 1, Page 2, etc in the spots where you think the page would start, and see how it reads. It may not end up like this as a finished book, but it really helps you get an idea of the flow of the book.

I even pretend to turn a page after reading a RHS page! Seriously. Just to see how long it takes to get to the next bit, and if that is a worthy place to do a page turn. This is really helpful in terms of timing.

If you read a story straight through on an A4 piece of paper, that is ***TOTALLY*** different to how it would be read in an actual book.

So they are some tips you can use to edit your picture books, some of which are slightly different to other genres. This is a MASSIVE advantage for us!

So take advantage of that advantage. Read it out as if there are page turns. Imagine the illustrations ... even if they're not what the final ones will be, it will still help you tighten your story and leave space for them.

And, most of all, as with all of this, play and have fun! We're writing picture books! Even the editing can be fun!

And now let's check out some of my favorite picture books and ones that feel to me like they are written, edited, illustrated and everything else really, really well!

SOME RECOMMENDED PICTURE BOOKS

To be honest, read whatever you want and whatever you can! Good picture books, bad picture books (*in your opinion*), long, short, rhyming, prose, whatever! See what works for you and what you like and what you hate and let that inspire your writing.

Try and figure out what the author's why may have been. Think about why they chose certain page turns, or left out bits you may have written.

And then check out some of these. They are picture books that have influenced me, and I think are brilliant for many reasons. Hopefully some of them connect with you as well.

STUCK by Oliver Jeffers. Amazing. Brilliant. Clever. Funny. Cute. I've talked about it enough already. Can't recommend it enough.

The Lorax by Dr Seuss. The way he uses language, and the way he writes rhyme is, in my opinion, unsurpassed. **He breaks the rules we are told are unbreakable** (*don't make up words, don't preach your message, word count, etc*), and he does it in a way that inspires and entertains. He's a genius, and when his books are still going strong 60 years after they were written, that's a pretty good sign he was something special.

Oh, the Places You'll Go by Dr Seuss. See **The Lorax**, but again, he breaks the rules in his rhythm and word use, and it works. He also gets a message in, and preaches it pretty strongly here as well. I know these two books are kind of obvious choices, but they're obvious for a reason. They're **INCREDIBLE!!!**

The Pinkish, Purplish, Bluish Egg by Bill Peet. He has a number of great books, but this is my favorite. A strong theme in Bill Peet's books is the thing that makes you an outcast can end up making you a hero. I heard something similar in a podcast, and I can't remember who was being quoted, but it was basically the things they sack you for when you're young are the things you get awards for when you're old.

If you take risks, it will freak some people out.

Take the risks anyway!

Piranhas Don't Eat Bananas by Aaron Blabey. This is a wonderful example of a fun story that kids ***LOVE!*** Read it and see if you can work out why, and then see if any of the things you notice are applicable to your stories.

The Short and Incredibly Happy Life of Riley by Colin Thompson. Beautiful, poignant, amazing. The life lessons are amazing, the pictures off-kilter and appealing because of that, and it's just so wonderful for adults as much as it is for kids.

QUESTIONS OFTEN FREQUENTED

DOES YOUR PICTURE BOOK NEED A MESSAGE?

Okay, so this is an interesting one. You will often hear from publishers that a picture book needs a message. You will ***also*** hear from publishers that you are not allowed to preach that message!

So where does that leave you?

Picture books **DO NOT** need a message. They don't. Kids get messages thrust at them left, right and center, from teachers, parents, other adults, everywhere. Sometimes a picture book **CAN JUST BE FOR FUN (***and will be inspiring in that***)!**

Also, in those fun books, you will very often be able to pull a message out of it if you need to, but don't make it forced. If you wrote a book that was designed simply to make kids laugh? ***PERFECT!***

In saying that, messages can also be wonderful in picture books. As mentioned earlier, they help kids talk about issues they otherwise would remain silent on.

So it's really up to you! If you have a message you would like to get across, put that message in there. But remember that this is a book, not a lesson. Reading a book should not only have children excited about that book, but excited about reading!

So give them entertainment as well as education. This doesn't mean it has to be funny, but it does have to be entertaining.

DO I INCLUDE ILLUSTRATION NOTES IN A PICTURE BOOK SUBMISSION?

Generally, the answer to this is no. Most illustrators don't like to be told what to draw, as it takes away the option of them seeing it visually.

However, if there is something you've written where a punchline to a joke would be a picture of something particular and there is no text for it (*ie the joke is that the T-rex EATS the tractor*), yes, do a note for that!

It will also often be written in a publisher's guidelines whether or not it is okay to include illustration notes. So check those, and if you are going to send illustration notes, it is good to send two documents. One with illustration notes, and one without. That way, the publisher can ignore them totally, I mean decide what version to send to the illustrator.

DO I INCLUDE PAGE NUMBERS IN A PICTURE BOOK SUBMISSION?

You don't have to, but you can. Again, the submission guidelines may specify, but it is up to you. I like to do it as **a)** it shows I have thought about things like page turns, number of words per page, etc and **b)** it shows I have seen the book as a book, rather than just a story.

Both these things are valuable for a publisher to know about you as a writer.

SHOULD I SEND IN PICTURES A FRIEND HAS DONE?

NO!!!!!

Unless your friend is James Hart or Heath McKenzie or Nicky Johnston or Leigh Hobbs or Serena Geddes or Oliver Jeffers, and the pictures are blow your mind incredible ... ***NO! NO NO NO NO NO!***

Even if it is one of those amazing illustrators, it's still almost a no. You can definitely say you have spoken to the illustrator and they are keen, but that's generally it.

Publishers have a stable of illustrators they turn to for a book, and they have an eye and an idea of which illustrator will fit which manuscript.

I have done submissions to publishers with James Hart, but that is because **a)** we are friends, and **b)** we had also already done a number of successful books together, so were seen as a team.

In a case like this, and especially if the illustrator has worked with that publisher before, it can be okay, but is still something to potentially discuss with the publisher first. If they are open to it, go for it. If not, don't!

WHAT ARE THE CHANCES OF BEING PICKED UP OFF THE SLUSH PILE?

Low. Like, really low. Rumor has it publishers publish around 2% of submissions from the slush pile.

And that rumor was a rumor I heard from publishers. Some are even **less than 2%!**

Scary, right?

Makes it seem impossible?

Maybe, but it doesn't have to. So how do you get around this scary number?

There are a few ways.

1. Download my free report on

5 Scary Numbers in Children's Book Publishing.

It looks at ways to overcome the slush pile and other scary numbers as well. **Scan the QR code** below or go to **www.adam-wallace-books.com/5-Scary-Numbers**

2. If you didn't download it (*what are you doing? Download it now! It's* **FREEEEEEE!**), here's a quick rundown to avoid the slush pile:

- Don't lock your work away. If no one sees it, no one publishes it.

- Don't lock your*self* away! Get amongst the kidlit community. It's amazing and supportive and awesome. And nearly every single book I have had published has come from a personal connection with the publisher.

- Get an Agent. This is hard, but not impossible. And agents immediately remove you from the slush pile.

- Say yes. At the start of your career, no matter how small the writing assignment, book launch, conference, whatever, say yes to it. You never know where it will lead.

- Self Publish. I did this to **a)** have a book, **b)** show publishers I had initiative and determination, and **c)** show publishers there was an audience for my writing.

- Get your work as good as it can possibly be. Be so good they can't ignore you. Etc, etc. None of the other stuff matters if your story stinks.

IS WRITING PICTURE BOOKS ONE OF THE FUNNEST THINGS EVER?

Yes. Yes it is. Absolutely and totally. It's awesome.

SECTION 12

And that was just the beginning ...

SUMMING UP

Yep, that's it. Our 152 page picture book journey is at an end ... sort of. I mean, I'm still talking.

Yeah, I haven't quite worked out that economy of words thing yet. That's why my first drafts are always so long, and then I get to cut it back into 500 words of amazingness.

It's also why my first three picture books were 900 words long! That was deliberate, to try and have a Dr Seuss feel to them, but it did take me a while to work out how to get a full story in under 500 words.

But that's the thing. We're always learning and writing and learning and growing and learning and thriving as artists.

And we ***need*** to keep growing, keep moving, keep flowing, never be stagnant, because if water becomes stagnant it stinks, and we don't want to be stinky!

So write and write and write and write and read and read and read and read and discuss and discuss and ***LISTEN*** and learn and grow and **always remember your why** and create with that in mind.

Why are you writing picture books?

If it's to entertain kids, **make sure your books are entertaining for kids.** Don't get caught up in what you ***think*** you should do, **write to your why.** If your why is to educate in an entertaining fashion, don't write boring education stuff!

Make it educational and make it fun!

And most of all ...

HAVE FUN YOURSELF!

You're making picture books, for crying out loud! You're bringing joy to children and parents and teachers, so

HAVE FUN WITH IT!

People often talk about how hard writing is, or how it's a slog, or work, or blah blah blah.

NO!

Writing is a privilege! And if people hate it so much, don't do it! No one's forcing you to - aside from when you're at school, or work, but we're talking about a whole different type of writing here!

You don't work the piano! You don't work a game! So don't work writing. Play! Have fun!

That energy will shine through your writing and/or illustrations, and you will enjoy the process so much more. That way, no matter what happens to your book after you write it, whether it gets published or not, sells millions or not, you will still have succeeded.

If writing still feels like a chore, reach back and find memories of the joy you got out of picture books as a kid, and focus that memory into your creating. Write real, and raw, and from your heart.

That's as good a starting point as any.

That way, your story has the freedom to go wherever your imagination takes it.

And if you do that, and writing ***still*** feels like a chore, well, you're in the wrong place.

Go do something else.

Thank you so much, keep creating, and I look forward to seeing your books on the shelves.

Adam Wallace

Made in United States
North Haven, CT
27 December 2024

63592249R00088